D1123381

The Illustrated
WINESPEAK

The Illustrated
WINESPEAK

RONALD SEARLE's
Wicked World
of
Winetasting

HARPER & ROW, PUBLISHERS, New York

Cambridge, Philadelphia, San Francisco,
London, Mexico City, São Paulo, Sydney

1817

FIRST U.S. EDITION

Library of Congress Cataloging in Publication Data

Searle, Ronald, 1920–
    The illustrated winespeak.

    1. Wine tasting. I. Title.
TP548.5.A5S43   1983   641.2′2′013   84-47597
ISBN 0-06-015320-2

The tortuous phrases that are frequently used when trying to describe music, fade into insignificance beside the agonising and often excruciating acrobatics of those whose duty it is to enlighten the baffled consumer regarding the more esoteric aspects of, say, Rotterdam rouge.

The art of wine-tasting has its own band of remarkable poets, those whose words vividly conjure up unimagined nuances and have us panting to experience the excitement and glow of drinking a particular bottle. Alas, they are as rare as the greatest vintages of the wines that dutifully pass their lips for our benefit.

The rest, that grotesque international band of snobbish inarticulate sponges, who are incapable of thinking beyond their incestuous little circles, do as much harm to the world of wine as they do to the language. Their day will come . . .

All the phrases in this little book have been plucked from unacknowledged but absolutely authentic sources. You could do worse than ponder over some of them. Cheers!

R.S.

Delightful bouquet

Gay and sprightly

Distinctive nose

Subtle and of great richness

Intense, aromatic, lots of body

Unusual

Pleasantly scented, very agreeable

Unpretentious

Notable in its category

Exceptionally full-bodied

Coarse but generous

Still green, but coming on nicely

Somewhat lacking in finesse

Delicately nuanced

A little sullen

Elegant, but lacks backbone

Ages beautifully

A pronounced scent of flowers

Surprisingly reticent

Round and supple

Full-bodied, with great character

Leave to age

Generous and high in alcoholic content

Lots of body, but supple

Vigorous and well constructed

Interesting depth of flavour

Delicate, supple and flowing

Overripeness coupled with some tartness

Lacks subtlety

On the light and forward side

Faint touch of bitterness

Haunting aroma

Dry, nervous, vigorous

A discernible touch of oak

Delightfully smoky aftertaste

Lots of class and much in demand

Really quite forward

Full, fruity character

Ripe, but lacks concentration

Will gain much charm with time

Has undergone noble rot

Healthy, but a bit sweaty

The nose is fantastic

Fullish body, but beginning to fade

Rather backward

Has voluptuousness and charm

in an earthy sort of way

Knit to a harmonious whole

Should remain in the cellar
for two or three years

Rather special